Kids Growing Up
Without a Home

THE CHANGING FACE OF MODERN FAMILIES

Kids Growing Up
Without a Home

Julianna Fields

Mason Crest Publishers, Inc.

MASON CREST PUBLISHERS INC.
370 Reed Road
Broomall, Pennsylvania 19008
(866)MCP-BOOK (toll free)
www.masoncrest.com

First Printing

9 8 7 6 5 4 3 2 1

ISBN 978-1-4222-1498-5
ISBN 978-1-4222-1490-9 (series)
Library of Congress Cataloging-in-Publication Data
Simons, Rae.

Produced by Harding House Publishing Service, Inc. www.hardinghousepages.com
Interior Design by MK Bassett-Harvey.
Cover design by Asya Blue www.asyablue.com.
Printed in The United States of America.

Although the families whose stories are told in this book are made up of real people, in some cases their names have been changed to protect their privacy.

Photo Credits

Creative Commons: d70focus 15, Folini, Franco 26;
Dreamstime: Absolut_photos 10, Images pgs 23, 32, 47

Contents

Introduction

The Gallup Poll has become synonymous with accurate statistics on what people really think, how they live, and what they do. Founded in 1935 by statistician Dr. George Gallup, the Gallup Organization continues to provide the world with unbiased research on who we really are.

From recent Gallup Polls, we can learn a great deal about the modern family. For example, a June 2007 Gallup Poll reported that Americans, on average, believe the ideal number of children for a family to have these days is 2.5. This includes 56 percent of Americans who think it is best to have a small family of one, two, or no children, and 34 percent who think it is ideal to have a larger family of three or more children; nine percent have no opinion. Another recent Gallup Poll found that when Americans were asked, "Do you think homosexual couples should or should not have the legal right to adopt a child," 49 percent of Americans said they should, and 48 percent said they shouldn't; 43 percent supported the legalization of gay marriage, while 57 percent did not. Yet another poll found that 34 percent of Americans feel a conflict between the demands of their professional life and their family life; 39 percent still believe that one parent should ideally stay home with the children while the other works.

Keep in mind that Gallup Polls do not tell us what is right or wrong. They don't report on what people should think—only on what they do think. And what is clear from Gallup Polls is that while the shape of families is changing in our modern world, the concept of family is still vital to our sense of who we are and how we interact with others. An indication of this is the 2008 Gallup poll that found that three out of four Americans reported that family values are important, while one in three said they are "extremely" important.

And how do Americans define "family values"? According to the same poll, here's what Americans say is their definition of a family: a strong unit where faith and morals, education and integrity play important roles within the structure of a committed relationship.

The books in the series demonstrate that strong family units come in all shapes and sizes. Those differences, however, do not change the faith, integrity, and commitment of the families who tell their stories within these books.

1 Families Without Homes

Terms to Understand

industrialized: having developed industries.

Great Depression: the period of economic crisis beginning with the stock market crash of 1929 and continuing through most of the 1930s.

precariously: uncertainly; being dependant on circumstances beyond one's control.

recession: a period of economic decline, less severe than a depression.

domestic violence: violence or abuse against a person within one's family or household.

chaotic: confused and disordered.

resilient: capable of recovering from hardship, disease, or other difficulties.

subsidized: partially paid for by a grant of money from the government or an agency.

If you were to drive through one of California's state parks, you might notice that twelve families have set up camp there. But they're not on vacation. These families (with their thirty-five children) are there because they have nowhere else to live. The park costs $8 a day, $240 a month—cheaper than any apartment or boarding house. Electricity isn't included, unfortunately, but toilets and showers are. For the families who live there, camping in the park is better than living on the street or in an abandoned building.

Eight of the families have at least one member who's employed. Two recently lost their jobs. Two families are receiving public assistance. One family is living in a tent, one is living in a car, and the rest have trailers. Several of the families received their trailers from Habitat for Humanity. For all of them, the state park is home now; after they pay for the park, for their food, gas, and clothing, there's not much left to put aside toward a permanent home. They plan on the park being their home for the foreseeable future.

Homeless families are about 34% of the total homeless population.

Meanwhile, on the other side of the country in Newark, New Jersey, Maryann Stebbins and her two little boys are living in their Dodge van. Maryann parks the van somewhere different every day, hoping to avoid the police telling her to move along in the middle of the night. She and the boys wash in public restrooms. Maryann's husband took off suddenly more than a year ago, and Maryann hasn't heard from him since; when she

Habitat for Humanity

Habitat for Humanity International provides "simple, decent, and affordable" housing for those in need. The group was founded in 1976 to help meet the housing needs of the world's poor. Their model is "partnership housing": Habitat volunteers build the house free of charge for a person or family in need who then moves in and begins making payments on the no-profit mortgage. Since their founding, Habitat has built or rehabilitated over 300,000 houses, most of them since 2000.

The 2004 U.S. Conference of Mayors Study (USCM) found that families with children make up about 30–40% of the homeless population in major cities of the United States.

lost her job six months ago, she could no longer make her mortgage payments, and the bank reclaimed her house. She's been working at a temp agency, making just enough money to cover food, gas money, and the monthly payments on the van.

These are true stories. They describe ordinary families, coping with life the best they can. They don't have a home now, but they did once. They've crossed the

line between those with homes and those without—and they've found out just how thin and flimsy that line really is, how easy it is to slip across it, and how hard it is to cross back the other way.

In the United States today, these families are not as unusual as they may seem. Thousands and thousands of families are without homes. In fact, among the *industrialized* nations, the United States has the largest number of homeless women and children. Not since the *Great Depression* have so many families been without homes.

How Many Are Homeless?

Since the early 1980s, estimates of the size of the overall homeless population have ranged from 192,000 to three million. This range of estimates is caused by the fact that there are different definitions of homelessness.

Two groups of individuals can be included in a definition of the homeless. The first is often called the "literally homeless," people who have no permanent homes and spend the night in places such as the street, cars, or emergency shelters. The other group sometimes considered homeless is the "*precariously* housed" population. People who are precariously housed are in danger of becoming literally homeless because they have no place of their own to live, or their current housing situation is tenuous. This group includes, among others, people who are doubled up—those who are living for short pe-

Approximately 1.35 million children will experience homelessness over the course of a year.

11

On any given day, researchers estimate that more than 200,000 children have no place to live.

riods of time with friends or relatives and thus lack a fixed, regular nighttime residence.

Children often appear among the precariously housed population because parents who become homeless may place their children with friends or relatives in order to avoid literal homelessness for them. Because some individuals and families choose to share housing as a regular, stable, and long-term arrangement, distinguishing the precariously housed from those in stable sharing arrangements is difficult.

Why Are Families Homeless?

A family may lose their home for a wide range of reasons. They may be extremely poor, but this is not always the case. Sometimes, there is simply not enough affordable housing to go around. The world is facing a time of economic *recession*, and this has immediate consequences for families. The gap between housing costs and income is widening. At the same time, many businesses are in trouble, and jobs are being cut. More and more families find themselves unable to meet their most basic financial needs.

When a family faces internal stress—such as illness, *domestic violence*, substance abuse, or divorce—their income level often goes down as well. Some families have safety nets that get them through these times of crisis—a network of family and friends that can help them out, savings in the bank, or other resources to which they can turn—but if a family has a weak safety net, or no safety net at all, even a relatively minor crisis can shove them out into the streets.

What Are Homeless Families Like?

The typical homeless family is a single mother in her late twenties with two children. This "typical" woman has already gone through a lot in life: she may have been abused as a child; she probably has had limited educational opportunities; she is often isolated and lonely. Homelessness adds to all the stresses she's already faced. She may feel like a failure for not being able to take care of her children better. She'll probably feel angry, guilty, sad, scared, and hopeless, all at the same time. No one could blame her for these emotions—but they can get in the way of her ability to take care of both herself and her children. So much trauma in her life also makes her more vulnerable to illness.

Children without homes face even greater threats to their well-being than their mothers do. Imagine being a young child who has to sleep in a different place every few nights. Think how scary it would be to lose the place that was most familiar to you—and at the same time know that your parents are powerless to cope with these frightening changes in your life. Even if a child's own family is relatively stable and secure, living on the streets or in shelters often means she will be exposed to people and circumstances other children don't usually face.

One-fifth of all jobs In the United States (24 million jobs) do not pay enough to keep a family of four out of poverty.

As of 2009, the federal minimum wage in the United States is $5.85 per hour (some states have higher minimum wages), which still leaves even a single full-time wage earner living below the Federal Poverty Line—$21,200 for a family of four, $17,600 for a family of three, and $14,000 for a family of two. On average, families need an income twice as high as the Federal Poverty Level to meet their most basic needs.

Homelessness brings with it a constant stream of stress and trauma that can have deep and lasting effects on children's intellectual and emotional development. Their physical development can be affected as well. Like their mothers, homeless children are also more apt to get sick. Hunger is an all-too-common experience in their lives.

All children experience many fears, but for a child without a home, the world looks truly dangerous and threatening. One research study found that 87 percent of all homeless children worry every day that something bad will happen to their families.

Homeless families, both adults and children, are stressed in one way or another. Most have lost their privacy and sense of security, along with their homes. Many double-up in overcrowded apartments with relatives or friends. Some sleep in cars or tents. Families who end up in a shelter have to adapt to surroundings that are usually noisy, overcrowded, and chaotic.

Often, homeless families are separated from each other; children may be sent to stay with relatives; older children are sometimes forced to strike out on their own; fathers and mothers often go separate ways.

Human beings are *resilient*, though, and in the face of these odds, many homeless families do find the strength to rebuild their lives. Often, the people without homes who find their way back to a more secure life are the ones who have come to rely on new "family" networks.

Homelessness is a complicated and enormous problem. Most of us can do very little to fight the circumstances that make homelessness more likely. And yet the families and individuals who have shared their stories in the chapters that follow demonstrate the power of ordinary human kindness. People who had little themselves cared enough to reach out and help. These stories show us that when we realize we are all part of a single human family, we have the power to build a world that will shelter those who have no homes.

According to the U.S. Department of Health and Human Services, over a five-year period, about 2–3 percent of the U.S. population (5–8 million people) will experience at least one night of homelessness.

Fifteen percent of all American families and 32% of single-parent families lived below the Federal Poverty Line in 2006. Among the nation's working families, 10 million are poor or nearly poor.

HEADLINES

("From "Study Reveals 'Hidden Homeless' in Rural America" by Clarke Canfield, *The Wichita Eagle*, June 6, 2009.)

The old, run-down trailer in the backcountry near Norridgewock wasn't much to look at, but it was home.

That was before the landlord died, setting in motion events that left Michelle DeStoop, Bobby Landry and their six children without a place of their own.

After losing their home, they sold their car to a junkyard when they couldn't afford to have it repaired. Without a car, they couldn't get around. Low on money, they lost their meager possessions when they couldn't pay the bill for storage.

Homelessness often means life in soup lines and on city streets, but as a new study commissioned by the state shows, it isn't confined to cities. It also can be found across rural areas, so concealed that some people are surprised it exists at all, the study finds.

. . . Many of the rural homeless stay at shelters—just like their urban counterparts—but some counties don't even have shelters, forcing the homeless to live in encampments, abandoned buildings, barns or cars. Many move from place to place, sleeping on a friend's or relative's couch or floor until they move on to the next person willing to take them in for a while.

All told, 1,200 people sought help at Maine's rural shelters last year, but the number of rural homeless is thought to be much higher. Of those who were looked at for the study, 97 percent had mental illness, 18 percent were alcohol abusers and 16 percent were drug abusers. Eleven percent were veterans.

DeStoop, 30, and Landry, 44, lived a simple life in the two-bedroom trailer they rented along Route 139 in Norridgewock, a town of 3,300 in central Maine. She worked in a dining hall at Colby College in Waterville; Landry, who is disabled and can't read or write, tended to things at home.

They lived next door to her mother's trailer and adjacent to an old roller skating rink that had been converted to a flea market. A farm down the road sold fresh produce in the summer months.

But when the trailer owner died, his heirs evicted them, removed the trailers and sold the property. At first, DeStoop and her family shared a house with her mother in Waterville. But after her mother moved out, it wasn't long before they followed—not able to pay the rent, heat and electricity on their own.

They bounced between her mother's and her grandfather's small apartments. But relationships can become strained when so many people live in such cramped quarters, so the family moved to Brunswick—where

Fifty-three percent of homeless mothers do not have a high school diploma.

17

Over 92% of homeless mothers have experienced severe physical and/or sexual abuse during their lifetime.

they eventually sought refuge at the Tedford Housing family shelter and have lived for eight months now. Moving an hour away meant DeStoop had to quit her job at the college.

Besides losing their home, their car and their possessions, DeStoop and Landry had three of their six children—ages 10, 8 and 6—taken by the state and put into a foster home, she said. The other kids—ages 4, 5 and 8—live with them at the shelter.

Last winter, Landry had to leave the shelter and spend more than three months on the streets because of a state investigation into their children's welfare. When he couldn't hook up with friends, he slept behind trash bins and in a gazebo on the town common, with a blanket to keep him warm.

He hit bottom in April when—in despair over his situation—he slashed his arm repeatedly with a razor blade to take his own life.

He was hospitalized overnight, and by coincidence was cleared by state investigators the very next day, setting the stage for his move back to the shelter, said Landry, the slash marks clearly visible on his arm.

"It's depressing. Very depressing," Michelle said. She later added: "You just keep your head up and keep on trying."

Michelle DeStoop is hopeful for the future. She's been told that she is near the top of the waiting list for *subsidized* housing and thinks she and her family could be in a home of their own this summer.

Any home is better than being homeless, she said.

Even a dilapidated trailer from the 1970s on a country road in the middle of nowhere.

"We were living there," she said. "We called it home."

Forty-four percent of homeless mothers lived outside their homes at some point during childhood. Of these women, 20% had been placed in foster care.

What Do You Think?

Is there a difference between a "home" and a "place to stay"? If so, how would you describe the differences? In what ways are the people described in this news article like the "typical" homeless person described earlier in this chapter? In what ways are they different? How is homelessness the same in rural areas as it would be in the city? How do you think it might be different?

2 Finding Their Way Home

The Koflan family—father Mike, mother Christine, son Michael, and daughter Katie—struggled like most American families. Both parents worked and lived from paycheck to paycheck. But they managed to stay afloat, with food reliably appearing on the table at dinnertime every day. First, disability hit the family—and then one day their life together was shattered, sending Mike in one direction, Christine and Katie in another, and Michael still another. None of them had a permanent address any longer. A stranger—a recovering alcoholic, as it happened—took a chance to help the family get a roof over its head again.

The year you turn eighteen, what do you expect to happen? Maybe you're counting on going to college. Or maybe you plan to get a job. Either way, you probably expect that your family will be there to help you, in one way or another, as you make the transition into adulthood.

Michael Koflan's family wasn't able to help him out when it came time for him to head out on his own. His family was evicted from their apartment a week after his eighteenth birthday. They did the best they could for him, but ultimately, he was adrift in the world, struggling to find his way.

It wasn't his family's fault. They had paid their rent, but the landlord hadn't paid the mortgage. Now the landlord had their cash, and they had a notice telling them they had two weeks to leave. They had no money in the bank for a down payment or a first month's rent, and nobody would rent them another apartment. They had knocked on the doors of several local social service agencies, but each one had a list of reasons it couldn't help.

But ready or not, the Koflans had to go. When the sheriff's deputies appeared at the door and told them they had thirty minutes to get out, they knew they couldn't postpone the inevitable anymore.

Michael's mom and little sister went to stay with a friend who had a spare bedroom. His father went to

> ### Terms to Understand
>
> ***consistency:*** following a set pattern that can be relied on.
> ***leniency:*** being tolerant or merciful.
> ***nonprofit agency:*** an organization that does not give extra profits to the owners or shareholders, but uses the money to help further its mission.
> ***supplement:*** to add to something to make it complete.
> ***increments:*** small amounts by which something grows or is added to.
> ***inundated:*** flooded, overwhelmed.
> ***hypothermia:*** abnormally low body temperature.

Eviction is when someone is kicked out of their residence by legal means. Although eviction rules vary from area to area, in most cases an eviction must follow a specific legal process. First, the landlord must give notice to the tenants, telling them what they are doing wrong (for example, they owe back rent), and how they can fix the problem and avoid eviction. If the problem is not solved, however, the landlord generally must serve a complaint, requiring than the tenant go to court, where the case will be determined by the judge. If the landlord wins, the tenant must leave the property by a certain date; otherwise they will be removed by a police officer.

stay at the YMCA. Michael was the child who was old enough to try to make it on his own.

Michael's mom had been the PTA president at school, and he had gotten good grades. But he dropped out now; later, he got his GED and a job assembling vacuum cleaners. It was a temporary job, though, and when they didn't need him anymore, he was let go.

Michael accepted his grandparents' invitation, and he and a friend headed to stay with them in their house in Florida. The boys planned to both get jobs and, within a short time, an apartment together. They would start a new life.

Things didn't turn out the way Michael had hoped, though. Michael did get a job, but his friend was gone within weeks, leaving Michael unable to afford rent on his own. The job was far from his grandparents' place, and it cost a small fortune to keep gas in the tank and maintain car insurance.

"And there are no buses like up here," he said. "You have to have a vehicle."

He got a promotion. Then his hours were cut. Not yet nineteen, he was discouraged with life.

When his grandparents went back North for the summer, he had little choice but to follow them. His dad was still at the Y; his mom and sister were at a women's shelter. There was still no place for Michael.

He had imposed on his grandparents long enough,

After a series of unfortunate events, Michael Koflan found himself living on the streets at just 18 years of age.

What Is the GED?

GED stands for General Educational Development—a series of five subject tests that certifies the taker has American or Canadian high school-level academic skills. To pass the GED tests, test takers must score higher than 40 percent of graduating high school seniors nationwide. Only individuals who have not earned a high school diploma may take the GED tests.

The tests were originally created to help veterans after World War II return to civilian life. More than 15 million people have received a GED credential since the program began. One in every seven Americans with high school credentials received the GED, as well as one in 20 college students.

In addition to English, the GED tests are available in Spanish, French, large print, audiocassette, and Braille.

Homeless children are four times more likely to have asthma.

he decided. The time had come for him to make it on his own. He stayed with friends, found jobs through a temp agency. Within months he was on the streets.

Here, in the city he had known all his life, surrounded by people he had known since he was born, he was suddenly homeless and nobody seemed to care.

"I thought I had a lot of friends, but after I lost all the material stuff, they were nowhere to be found," he said.

Back when he had dropped out of high school, he had walked much of the city looking for a job. He remembered seeing several abandoned buildings. Some of them, he knew, were used by drug dealers, but there was one in an old industrial area, near occupied houses in a working-class neighborhood. He found a way in—and claimed it as his new home.

"I didn't know about food pantries and soup kitchens back then," he said. "I was hungry all the time. Eventually, I did start going to the pantries—but they gave out a bunch of canned food, and I had no way to open it."

Every day he crawled in a window of that abandoned building after dark and left before dawn. "I didn't want to get arrested for trespassing," he said.

If he found a dollar, he nursed a cup of coffee at McDonald's for as long as he could, then spent the day job hunting and at the public library. There he read books on survival. He learned tricks like filling empty soda bottles with hot water in service-station rest rooms, and tucking them around the edges of his blankets for warmth when he slept.

"Contrary to what people believe, unheated buildings aren't warmer than the outdoors," he said. "I can honestly say it was colder inside."

By age twelve, 83% of homeless children had been exposed to at least one serious violent event. Almost 25% have witnessed acts of violence within their families. Children who witness violence are more likely than those who have not to be aggressive and/or fearful, and to have higher levels of depression and anxiety. They may have a greater acceptance of violence as a means of resolving conflict.

He made his blankets into a tent and warmed the air inside with a candle until he could no longer breathe. From mid-October until the end of December, he slept wadded up in his covers.

According to the USCM, applicants must wait an average of 20 months for public housing, so many homeless people end up sleeping on the street, in a car, or in an abandoned building.

"Fortunately it didn't snow until January," he commented.

The job hunt was frustrating. He needed a permanent address to give potential employers, not to mention a phone number at which they could call him—but he had neither. He was still trying to get a room in a local shelter, but they were all full.

By then he had discovered soup kitchens, and he walked miles to whichever part of town had one that day. "But I never stole," he said with pride. "There were times I did consider going to jail. On purpose. But I had hope eventually an opportunity might come through. But it was amazing I managed to hold onto my morals."

He was hanging on by an emotional thread when a friend said, "Wait another week and see what happens."

That's when one company came through for him. It was only a temporary job, but it got him into an apartment with a friend.

He learned a lot through the experience, he said. "I spent a lot of time thinking, 'I can't believe I'm in this situation' and slowly moved to 'What can I do to change it?'—since then I've been a big believer in positive thinking."

"You do the same thing over and over and stay in the same rut, or you realize that doing anything else might lead to something positive," he said.

> Children experiencing homelessness are sick four times more often than other children. They have four times as many respiratory infections; twice as many ear infections; and five times more stomach problems.

Children experiencing homelessness have three times the rate of emotional and behavioral problems compared to non-homeless children.

He encountered a lot of apathy—and the occasional kindness—and is convinced that people just don't understand how deep desperation can be.

Now that he has seen the worst life has to offer, he's not willing to settle for just a job to keep food on the table. He wants to be happy.

He can fix computers, for example, but he doesn't like to. He wants to work with people in the years to come.

"A lot of people suffer and don't know why," he says "If I have the answer, I should give it to them."

He applied for a job training program that will give him a start in nursing. "I have no doubt in my mind I can convince them to give me this opportunity," he said. "I'm ready for it and I'm going to run with it all the way."

HEADLINES

(From "Homeless Students in Fairfax Schools up 25 Percent," *Fairfax County Times*, November 19, 2008.)

The number of homeless students in Fairfax County Public Schools is up 25 percent from last year, primarily due to home *foreclosures*.

Kathi Sheffel has been the homeless liaison for FCPS for the last eight years.

Under a provision of the No Child Left Behind Act of 2001, school districts are required to have a homeless liaison to help "highly-mobile" students maintain their educational requirements with as little disruption as possible.

Sheffel receives an annual federal grant of $97,000 to help supply her office with a full-time social worker, a part-time administrative assistant, and 21 part-time tutors for homeless students.

"We try to eliminate any barriers to their enrollment and education by providing support in lots of different ways," Sheffel says. "We want to make sure these kids don't get lost during their homelessness."

. . . Title X, Part C of the No Child Left Behind Act defines a homeless student as living in an emergency or transitional shelter; a motel, hotel, or campground; in a car, a park, public place; bus or train station; abandoned building or doubled up with relatives or friends due to a lack of a fixed, regular, and adequate nighttime residence.

According to Sheffel, there are nearly 1200 students in Fairfax County schools this year that meet that definition. That is an almost 25 percent increase from last year, when the number was only 900.

Among young homeless children, one out of five (between three and six years of age) have emotional problems serious enough to require professional care.

Among school-age homeless children, 47% have problems such as anxiety, depression, and withdrawal, compared to 18% of other school-age children.

Asked why the numbers have increased so dramatically, she gives a one-word answer: "foreclosures."

"I have been here for eight years and the numbers have increased every year, but this is not usual to have this many in such a short period," she said.

Sheffel receives calls stemming from foreclosures on a daily basis and her phone is ringing off the hook.

"I get calls from schools every day saying that a student's family is being evicted later in the week," she says. "Many come from families being evicted because their landlords are being foreclosed upon."

Many of these families wind up taking temporary residence in one of the county's four local family shelters. But according to Belinda Buescher of the Department of Family Services, nearly 100 families are currently on a waiting list because the shelters are currently full.

"The stress on a child in a homeless situation is phenomenal," said Sheffel. "The stress of not knowing where they are going to be staying, whether or not they will be able to remain together, if their parents will be OK and if they can stay in their school, can really take their toll. We try our best to minimize that stress."

What Do You Think?

Why do you think the number of foreclosures has risen so much? If you were to lose your home, how would that affect your ability to do well in school? List as many ways as you can.

Children experiencing homelessness are four times more likely to show delayed development. They also have twice the rate of learning disabilities as non-homeless children.

Christine Koflan can't count how many addresses she has had over the last three years. Many of them lasted

Mothers experiencing homelessness often struggle with both physical and mental health issues.

- They have three times the rate of post-traumatic stress *disorder* (36%) and twice the rate of drug and alcohol dependence (41%).
- About 50% of mothers have experienced a major depressive episode since becoming homeless.
- Over one-third have a *chronic* physical health condition, such as asthma or high blood pressure.
- They have ulcers at four times the rate of other women.
- Twenty percent have anemia, compared to 2% of other women under age 45.

After moving from one temporary place to another, Christine and Katie Koflan were rescued by the kindness of Angel Pereira. With his help, they found an apartment and were reunited with Katie's father.

only a month or two before she and her daughter Katie had to move on.

Before that, it was just one address, for a decade and a half, with her husband and two children. But when that situation ended, she was scrambling for sure footing—and couldn't find it.

Christine's childhood had been less than stable, too. She lived with both her divorced parents at different times, and her mom had moved so often—forcing Chris-

The YMCA and YWCA

The YMCA (Young Men's Christian Association) movement began in London in 1844, seven years later, the first American YMCA started in Boston. These early Ys were "fellowships" for young men seeking "spiritual and mental improvement" through prayer, Bible study, lectures, and good works. During the Civil War, the YMCA provided social services for Union soldiers, and after the war the YMCA added "social and physical improvement" to its statements of purpose.

By the beginning of the twenty-first century, the American YMCA was part of an international association representing YMCAs in 120 countries.

Meanwhile, the YWCA, originated with a "Ladies Christian Association" founded in New York City in 1858. This first YWCA opened a boarding house for young women as well as a day-nursery. Focusing on female empowerment, it addressed many social issues including racism, peace, and voter education. Based in New York, the YWCA by 2000 had 326 local associations in every state and was affiliated with the World YWCA operating in 101 countries.

Both the YWCA and the YMCA have been active around the world in fighting homelessness. Most Ys provide affordable housing—what is often referred to as "transitional" housing, meant to offer short-term solutions for families seeking a more permanent residence.

The average wait for public housing (subsidized by the government so that rents are much lower than average) is twenty months.

tine to change schools so often—that Christine dropped out and moved in with her first boyfriend when she was fifteen. They later married, then divorced.

Then she met Mike, the man with whom she'd spend most of her life. They married and had two children. She and her husband both worked full-time jobs, and she did catering on the side. He had worked sanitation for the city, then got a job moving used cars around a dealer's lot. They had a van, a big TV, a solid life.

But when Mike developed back problems and ended up on disability, the weight of the family fell on her

Food Pantries

Food pantries are nonprofit organizations operated as part of a church, government or community group that distribute emergency food to families and individuals. Food pantries receive their supplies from food banks, which in turn get food from companies or supermarkets, as well as donations from individuals. The U.S. government and state governments also contract with food banks to distribute USDA surplus commodities and FEMA food. Food banks distribute goods such as canned and boxed dry groceries, fresh produce, frozen foods, bakery products, and some personal hygiene or household cleaning products.

shoulders. Bills piled up. The utilities were shut off, turned back on, shut off again.

Christine had never been in robust health, even when she was younger. The growing stress on her tipped her frail *constitution* over the edge and she could no longer hold down a job either. Her doctor said that Christine had a large cluster of health issues, but he couldn't tell her how she could feel better again.

She went from doctor to doctor, trying to find answers. The answers never came, but the bills did. Not having insurance coverage or money, she could only ignore the mounting pile of invoices for medical services rendered. Eventually, the bills went into *collection*, and marks against the family's name blackened still more pages of their credit report. As if all that wasn't enough, their van was stolen after they had put their last dollars into fixing it.

When they were forced to leave the apartment they had lived in for fifteen years, the family had to separate to keep from literally living on the streets. Her husband went to a YMCA while Christine and Katie began the revolving-door craziness that characterized their life for the next three years. Their son Michael's story was told earlier in this chapter, but Christine and Kate had their own story.

Christine tried to find help from various social service agencies, but no one could provide the family with any long-term answers. Instead, a few people

A person's credit rating indicates his or her ability to repay a debt. Credit rating is built up on the basis of the (1) credit history (how well you've repaid your bills in the past), (2) present financial position (how much you earn, how much savings you have), and the (3) likely future income. Special agencies collect, store, analyze, summarize, and sell such information. If you have a poor credit rating, banks and other financial institutions will be unlikely to give you a loan or a credit card account.

Eighty-four percent of homeless families are female-headed. This is due to a number of factors:

- Most single-parent families are female-headed (71%).
- Single-parent families are among the poorest in the nation and as such, are extremely vulnerable to homelessness.
- Many family shelters do not accept men into their programs, causing families to separate when they become homeless.

she calls "angels" stepped up. One, the mother of Katie's school friend, cleared out space in their family's apartment for Christine and Katie to have a place to sleep. That situation couldn't last forever, though, and it didn't. Soon mother and daughter needed another opportunity.

A social services agency found them another temporary home, this time in a local "inn" that housed *paroled* felons and other homeless people. Christine wasn't happy with the atmosphere there, not when she had Kate living with her too.

Then they got a room at the YWCA. Unfortunately, the old building was undergoing extensive renovations; Christine was allergic to the chemicals in the building materials. She was desperate to get out.

"I called every homeless shelter, but they only took men," she said.

She wanted to look for another place, but had no money for a bus pass—and out of the blue, another angel—this time an official at the transit authority—stepped up to give her one.

Meanwhile, another social services agency came up with a room for her. It, too, was in a building intended for ex-cons needing a new start in life. Desperate, mother and daughter stayed there until her Mike found himself a room in a local boarding house and told Christine another room would soon be open.

Parents and at least one of their children were re-united—even though they had to live in a rickety building next door to a facility warehousing sex offenders. A mattress on the floor was the bed mother and daughter shared for a year and a half. The only kitchen facilities were used by all the building's occupants, so Christine ate sandwiches or cooked their food in a toaster oven in her husband's room. Katie's beloved Barbie dolls stayed in bins stacked against a door.

This is the breakdown of the homeless population according to a 2008 report from the National Coalition for the Homeless.

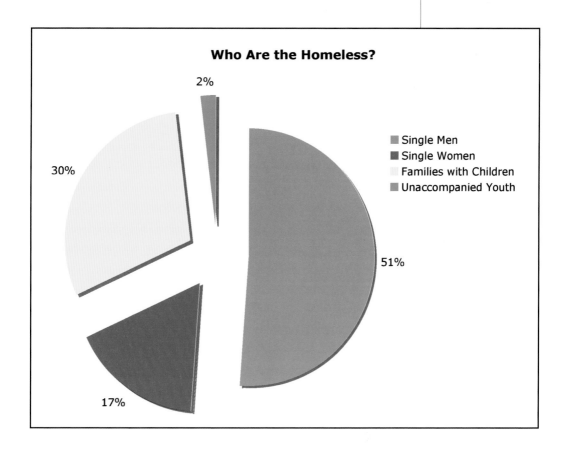

Who Are the Homeless?

2%

30%

51%

17%

- Single Men
- Single Women
- Families with Children
- Unaccompanied Youth

Through all those moves, Katie continued going to the same school. Experience had taught Christine the importance of **consistency** in that regard, and Katie's grades reflected the nurturing she received from her mother.

When the building became infested with roaches, the manager sprayed heavy-duty chemicals in all the nooks and crannies—and again Christine found herself gasping to breathe and needing another place to live. This time, options were fewer than ever. The family had "used up" all the help that social services and friends could offer.

Christine and Mike longed for their own apartment—but they had no money whatsoever for a security deposit and first month's rent. What's more, the utility company refused to give them a new account until they had paid off the balance on an old bill. And they didn't have beds to sleep on, even if they had been able to move to a real apartment.

This time a real angel came to the rescue, a Latino man named Angel who nagged Christine to remove Katie from an unhealthy environment. Angel (whose story is told in chapter 3) had seen enough in his own life to want a better circumstance for Christine and Katie.

Christine made up her mind to find an apartment, even though Mike was content to remain where they were. Angel accompanied her to see apartments for rent, pleading her case when she herself was too embarrassed to ask for

Of children in grades 3 through 12 who are homeless and participated in state assessment tests, only 48% were proficient in reading and only 43% were proficient in math.

leniency in paying the deposit. When one landlord finally agreed to help, Angel gave a $200 deposit and his name on the account so Christine could get utilities.

Now Katie would have her own room, and her Barbies could come out to play again. But even with the possibility of a nice new home so close at hand, Katie said she didn't want to move if it meant leaving her dad behind. So Mike moved with them. Now, with their combined disability checks, they would have enough to pay the rent.

A *nonprofit agency* set them up with free beds and other furniture, which were delivered to the family's new apartment. Other small nonprofits came up with blankets and household goods to *supplement* what the family had had to leave behind in its many moves.

They paid the security deposit in small *increments* over the next few months, and they shopped garage sales and went to food pantries. Slowly, they got on their financial feet again.

Christine began to feel safe for the first time in three years.

They got to know the neighbors, who would never have guessed that this perfectly "normal" family had been in the ranks of "the homeless" they heard so much about. After all, the homeless were only drunks and druggies—right?

Christine and her family knew better.

> Researchers have found that 1.7 million housing units (apartments or houses) are needed to fill the gap in affordable housing for extremely low-income households in the United States.

HEADLINES

(From "Schools, Agencies Seeing Big Increase in Homeless Families" by Kate Bolduan, CNN, May 2, 2009.)

Sheila Wash greets her son and daughter, 13-year-old Cecil and 9-year-old Sheliah, every day when their school buses arrive "home."

They talk about the school day, their homework and even joke that Sheliah can't remember what she ate for lunch. The fourth-grader wonders aloud, "What did we have? We had something good."

But it's hardly a homecoming for any of them.

The Wash family has been homeless since 2007, after Sheila lost her government job. She says unemployment benefits quickly ran out and, as she searched for a job, the family was forced to move six times in the last two years. They're now living in the Family Forward Shelter in Washington.

"I just thank God we have a roof over our head right now. You have to accept the things that come to you. You don't like them but, you know, until you can get your foot forward, you do what you have to do. We just keep going," Wash said.

Wash's situation was only made worse as the economic recession set in. Jobs became harder and

One in seven U.S. households—37.3 million—has severe housing cost burdens. Most of these households (78%) are in the bottom quarter of the income distribution (earning $23,000 or less a year).

harder to find with more competition for each position. She says she's still searching.

The Washes are part of the changing face of homelessness in America today. For years, homelessness has been depicted as that of an individual man or woman living on the street and begging for money. But with the perfect storm of the foreclosure crisis and the faltering economy, more and more families are becoming homeless. . . .

"People lose their jobs. Their monthly household expenses spiral out of control because maybe their car broke down that month, and when you have such a tight budget with high rental costs, there is no room for error. And so that is what really leads families to the shelter door," said Mary Cunningham, author of Preventing and Ending Homelessness—Next Steps.

Reflecting on their struggles over the last few years, Sheila calls it "eye-opening." "It's like they say you never know [someone] until you walk in their shoes, so truly I know now and if I ever get out [of] this situation, I will always give back to people less fortunate than I am because I know their struggles," Wash said.

School officials in Prince George's County, Maryland, where the two Wash children go to school, say

A full-time worker earning minimum wage cannot afford a one-bedroom apartment priced at the average rent anywhere in the United States. A full-time worker must earn at least $17.32 per hour to afford the average two-bedroom apartment.

Among all homeless women, 60% have children under age 18, but only 65% of them live with at least one of these children.

a day doesn't go by without the need to enroll another child as homeless. Denise Ross, supervisor for the school district's Homeless Education Office, said they've been inundated with requests.

"Some of them are embarrassed, some of them are scared, some of them are sad. They're just not sure what's going to happen next," Ross said. "Students who are displaced or homeless students feel that school is a safe haven. They really want to come to school. They really want to attend school."

For homeless students, Prince George's County Schools offers free transportation to and from school, free breakfast and lunch, help with school supplies and also clothing. "Either in the shuffle of being evicted or moving from shelter to shelter or place to place, their clothes may not have followed them. Or may have been set out and somebody may have taken them. So they may only have [the] clothes that are on their back. Our intent is always to provide them with at least three complete sets," Ross said.

Sheila Wash says school is not only important because of her children's education, but it has also been an important source of stability in their lives. "[A] very big help," she says. And help they still need with the obstacles ahead.

The Family Forward Shelter is a hypothermia shelter, only open through the winter, which means the Wash family needs to find another temporary home, and they haven't had much luck.

But with a smile that seems to never fade, 9-year-old Sheliah describes the one wish that keeps her family going. "I wish we had a house with a car," she says. "I pray that my mom, that we wake up in the morning and that [we] get a house and everything we wanted."

Among all homeless men, 41% have children under age 18, but only 7% live with at least one of their own children.

What Do You Think?

When Sheiliah grows up, how do you think she will look back on this time in her life? What will she tell her children?

3 Families Made on the Streets

Terms to Understand

multiple sclerosis: a chronic disease of the nervous system, causing a variety of symptoms involving the nerves or muscles.
amends: compensation for loss or damages.
functional: working.
rehab: short for "rehabilitation"; a program designed to get a person clean from alcohol or drugs or to restore them to health.
off the wagon: begin drinking alcohol again after a period of staying away from it.
solvency: the ability to pay one's debts.
coma: a long period of unconsciousness, together with lack of response to physical stimuli, from which a person cannot be awakened.

In one way or another, we all need our families. Try to imagine your life without your family. They may drive you crazy sometimes, but it's pretty hard to think of life without them. What would you do if you were all alone in life, without even a home of your own? It would be pretty lonely.

When you think of the word "family," an image of a mother, a father, and some kids probably comes to mind—people who live together, take care of each other, and rely on each other.

But families can be built on something other than a blood bond, and people who are homeless often find ways to fill the empty spots in their lives with a new family, created from whomever (and sometimes whatever) is handy. A man named

Angel Pereira reached out to others in trouble—people like Christine and Katie—and created family bonds that were stronger than the blood ones he had lost along the way. In the case of Arna O'Brien, friends and stray cats became her family—a group of beings she was committed to and that were committed to her.

Growing up, Angel Pereira had family in both his native Puerto Rico and Brooklyn. As a child he spent years bouncing between both places, staying with his father and grandparents on the tropical island and with his mother and stepfather in the Big Apple borough.

He started drinking at age thirteen—a bottle of Ballentine Ale once a week or so. Before long he was a full-blown alcoholic who avoided living on the streets only by drying out at one treatment center or another—only to return to the bottle again.

Terms to Understand

sobriety: the state of being sober, staying away from alcoholic drinks completely or only drinking them in moderation.
diversity: variety.
imperative: absolute necessity.
expenditures: expenses; the act of spending money.

For a long time, Angel, who stands only about five-foot-seven, felt like a big man. He was a gangbanger, hanging with the toughest of the tough on Brooklyn's streets where stabbings and shootings weren't headlines but just a way of life. "I smoked pot and drank but I was afraid of heroin," he said. "I'd see all these people I knew with track marks. They couldn't find a place to shoot anymore and they'd say, 'Angel, shoot me up.' I did, and they'd give me two marijuana cigarettes for it."

He had quit school and was part of a four-man rock-and-roll group that sang at weddings and other events. At twenty, he married a girl he had known most of his life. Inez was just seventeen at the time, but the couple was already building their family. Angel III was born the first year of their marriage, and two years later, baby Alice came along.

Angel didn't like watching his son play in the same tough streets he had, so he moved his family to Staten Island. "I didn't want the same for him as I had," Angel said.

After Alice was born, Inez began losing her balance and dropping things. Her sister dragged her to a clinic, and Inez was diagnosed with *multiple sclerosis*. "I saw that disease in every stage until she was a vegetable," Angel said, tears pooling in his eyes. In her thirties she entered a nursing home and the kids went to live with her mother, who had never approved of Angel.

By then he was at the bar whenever he wasn't at work. "I was used to going home to the kids and the wife and now I was alone," he said.

But he never stopped loving Inez. She died at age forty-five, and the day of her funeral was the last day Angel ever saw his kids. Angel's family was gone.

When he met Christine Koflan and her ten-year-old daughter Katie years later, he wanted to help them to make *amends* for what he hadn't done for his own daughter when he had been a younger man. He

Families of color are overrepresented in the homeless population:

- 43% are African-American
- 38% are White, non Hispanic
- 15% are Hispanic
- 3% are Native American.

had a lot of regrets, and alcohol had never managed to drown his sorrows.

"I was a *functional* alcoholic," he said. "Only the smell would tell you I was drunk; otherwise you wouldn't know."

He held good jobs, one for fifteen years, another for eight, another for five, but eventually alcohol got the best of him. "I knew plenty of drunks who lived on riverbanks and under viaducts, but I was too smart to be reduced to their level," he said. So every time he ran out of money to pay for an apartment, he'd check himself into *rehab*. Six months, later he'd be a new man, outfitted

Angel Pereira coped with the loss of his wife and children by drinking alcohol. After nearly dying, he went to rehab and now devotes his time to helping others who have found themselves on the streets.

in new clothes and with a new apartment waiting for him.

Pretty soon he'd be selling his food stamps for cash to buy another bottle, then another. And then back into rehab he'd go.

When he finished drying out at Salvation Army one time, they were so impressed with him, they offered him a job on staff. He would have free use of an efficiency

Like many homeless people, Arna has discovered a new definition for the word "family."

apartment for three months and free meals while drawing a decent salary—and then they'd help him get a nice apartment where he would pay the rent. Good deal, he thought, and he started saving his paychecks. He liked his job and had $3,000 in the bank when he moved into a beautiful studio apartment. "I was doing good there," he says. "Then one Friday night I got drunk."

That was all it took to knock him *off the wagon*, out of the job and into rehab again.

When he got out, he still had money in the bank—and he knew full well what money could buy. He bought bottles for all his friends—and when the money ran out, he checked himself into treatment again, just before he got evicted.

That was the pattern of Angel's life: in and out of *solvency*, in and out of rehab, on and off the wagon—until one day he drank himself into an eight-day *coma* and very nearly died.

That did it. He was done with drinking. He was sixty-four and had been an alcoholic more than half of his life.

Today, he has a room in a boarding house and money in his pocket. He takes a drink once in a while, he admits, but he knows he can go downhill fast if he's not careful. He has "brothers" on the street still, but he doesn't visit their camps; he knows it would be too dangerous to his precarious *sobriety*. It's dangerous in other ways, too.

Supplemental Security Income (SSI) is a federal income supplement program funded by general tax revenues. It is designed to help aged, blind, and disabled people, who have little or no income; and it provides cash to meet basic needs for food, clothing, and shelter.

Natural disasters can plunge whole communities into homelessness. This is what happened in the United States after Hurricane Katrina, and it continues to happen around the world, whenever an earthquake, tsunami, hurricane, or other natural disaster destroys homes. People who are poor are especially vulnerable, since a natural disaster can wipe out not only their home but their means of livelihood, leaving them no resources for recovery.

"If somebody has money and falls asleep, they'll go through your pockets," he said. "They'll take your socks and leave your shoes on." At that he laughs—he was making a joke—but then says that he slept with his shoes and socks as a pillow in every rehab he was ever in, because the other guys would steal them if you left them unattended.

On the street, when a drunk gets his check from the government, he's suddenly the object of intense scrutiny. "He goes to the bank, cashes the check, gets drunk. And they're all watching him and waiting till he passes out, and they go through his pockets to take all his money."

One friend died in a homeless camp last winter. He had been drinking and the alcohol made him feel warm, Angel said. So he fell asleep and froze to death without ever waking up.

No homeless camps for Angel. He was always too smart for that, and now, maybe he'll be smart enough to appreciate what's left of his life. One thing he's sure of: he's part a family now, a family of people who know how easy it is to cross the line between safety and the streets. Angel does his best to help this family of his by doing what he can to help people like Christine and her family. He also donates his time to run a local canteen that feeds people who are facing similar troubles.

Angel knows family has to stick together.

HEADLINES

(From "Handling America's Homeless Families" by Doug Bandow, *Washington Times*, May 17, 2009.)

With the economy in apparent freefall, human needs, including homelessness, have grown. Our starting point should be moral, not political. . . . Matthew quotes Jesus as telling the sheep: "For I was hungry and you gave me something to eat, I was thirsty and you gave me something to drink, I was a stranger and you invited me in." They ministered to Jesus by doing these things "for one of the least of these brothers of mine."

This duty cannot be subcontracted to government. The Bible demonstrates concentric rings of responsibility moving outward, starting with individuals who are enjoined to take care of themselves, rather than living off of others. Those who fail to care for their families are worse than unbelievers, Paul warns. The early church transferred money within and among faith communities. Finally, Paul says in Galatians, "let us do good to all people."

Good people in a good society take care of those in need.

If the political authorities are to act, it should be because other institutions have failed to meet people's basic needs. Today, far more private than public programs serve the homeless. . . .

Diversity of responses is particularly important in dealing with a problem as complicated as homelessness. . . . The answer is not simply more money for more government programs, of which there are thousands nationwide. This enormous challenge can be best met by reflecting back on the biblical model. We need to simultaneously meet current needs, which often include illness and hunger, and reduce future problems.

First, individuals and families have a moral as well as practical *imperative* to behave responsibly. Americans need to relearn how to resist substance abuse, curb wasteful *expenditures* and save money. Borrowers and lenders alike should spend money wisely.

Second, family and friends, backed by churches and other social networks, should be the first line of defense to homelessness. The need may be as simple as temporary financial aid or an empty couch. Such informal assistance can soften the impact of unexpected hardship while preserving the dignity of those in need.

Third, private social programs are better than government initiatives in ministering to the whole person, rather than treating those in trouble as numbers and prescribing only a check or bed. Some of the neediest require proverbial "tough love"—compassion and discipline. It is important to keep people off the street and ensure that they won't face the same problem again. That often requires changes in behavior as well as circumstance. . . .

Fourth, local initiatives are most likely to be effective in meeting needs that vary dramatically by region. Unfortunately, the results of many of the federal welfare programs, including those directed at housing, ranging from rental vouchers to Section 8 to public housing, have been ugly. The government's safety net is best maintained by states and localities rather than by Washington.

Good people in a good society take care of those in need. That includes the homeless. But just as the problem is complex, so is the solution. And we will do best if we respond first at a human rather than at a political level.

What Do You Think?

Describe who the author of this article believes should be helping the homeless. Who does he think should NOT be involved with helping the homeless? Do you agree with him or disagree? Why?

Arna O'Brien has learned some of the same lessons about family that Angel has. She knows that family is really the only warmth and safety you can count on in this cold world.

Her understanding of this most basic fact began on a chilly, dark day when she stood all alone in a trailer that reeked of cat urine.

When Arna had moved out, she had left the cat door in place. The cats—six or seven of them, or maybe eight—weren't pets so much as regular guests that came and went as they pleased. None of them had ever seen the inside of a veterinarian's office. They had been born in the surrounding woods, where they fed on mice, birds, and other small creatures. They'd slept on her couch sometimes while she watched TV, then returned to the woods.

She couldn't take them with her when she went to live with her friend, but she wanted them to still be able to sleep on the couch whenever they wanted. They were, after all, her closest family.

The trailer was trash by then anyhow. Floodwaters from a nearby creek had washed it off its foundation and bent it like a paperclip. Now the ceiling leaked and wind wailed through gaps around the windows. Muddy water had oozed up through the floor, soaking everything in its path. Her furniture, which had never been luxurious, became sodden garbage. The couch smelled, as did everything else, but it had dried and the cats didn't seem to mind.

So she had left the trailer—and now, two years later, with nowhere else to go and winter snows already flying, she had to move back in.

She was sixty-four, disabled, and alone.

Life had never been easy for Arna. Her dad had been a truck driver and her mom a nurse's aide, but as hard as they worked, they could never actually make ends meet. Arna and her five siblings had eaten a lot of hotdogs and beans, and they didn't go hungry very often. Cheap food, used clothes, an old truck that gave out as much as it ran: that was the family's lot in life. But they had a roof over their head on a small farm and, for better or worse, they were together. One by one they dropped out of high school, went off and got married. Their lives would take them in such separate directions that they barely communicated as the years rolled on.

"I quit school at the ninth grade, then went working to help Mom and Dad," Arna reported. "Then I got married."

Arna's marriage wasn't a happy one. Her husband James struggled with depression and self-medicated with alcohol. Community mental health services could have helped him, but he didn't want anything to do with them. So he stayed in bed a lot, snarled at Arna a lot, and had trouble keeping a job. He jerry-rigged some repairs around the old trailer, but they mostly didn't last.

At age thirty-nine he killed himself, leaving Arna alone—but for the cats.

Her father had taught her how to drive a truck. She never got her CDL (commercial driver's license) but started hauling loads in box trucks from here to there across the region. She got training to be a nurse's aide, too. "So I worked the same jobs as my mom and dad," she said.

When a disabled friend needed a place to live, Arna welcomed Diana into the trailer. Soon Arna, too, was disabled. Problems with her back and legs left her barely able to walk. Together, the two women struggled to get by on small checks that came every month from the government. But they were okay. The two of them, plus the menagerie of cats, made a family. Their needs were simple and they got by.

Then came the floods in 2006.

The women grabbed what they could as water crept up inch by inch until they had to wade in knee-deep water to get out the door. They threw everything into Arna's old truck and took off for a nearby shelter.

But after that . . . neither woman was sure what should come next.

Diana eventually went into a nursing home to accommodate her ever-increasing need for care. Arna stayed with one set of friends, then another. They were the only "family" she had to lean on during these desperate times.

By late fall 2008, those friends had decided to move South, and Arna was left with no place to live. Again she stashed her possessions into the truck—and headed for the trailer, alone.

Public concern about homelessness in the United States has increased in recent years. A 1995 Gallup poll found that 86% of Americans feel sympathy for the homeless, and 33% report that they feel more sympathy now than they did five years ago. According to the same poll, one reason for this apparent increase in sympathy is that 17% of Americans, primarily women and young adults, believe that they could become homeless.

Now she had to push her way through two years' growth of weeds just to get to the front porch. Her foot caved through the rotten wood when she stepped onto it. The key still worked in the lock, though, and when she opened the door a new batch of cats scrambled out the window.

It was a warm day for November, and sun shone in the windows to give her light. The place was a disaster, having been home to not only the cats but all manner of foraging animals. Their claws had ripped open the cupboards, sending the contents into heaps on the floor.

She wadded newspaper into the cracks around the windows, put buckets where water dripped down from the ceiling. The furnace had died in the flood, but she poured propane into two space heaters and got the place up past 50 degrees in no time.

Her bed had been spared in the flood. Not wanting to think how many animals might still be living deep in its mattress, she pulled a comforter over it, piled blankets on top of herself, and fell asleep.

She lived like that for two months. In the midst of all her misery, she was happy to be reunited with the cats – and to make the acquaintance of those who had moved in while she was gone.

In Arna's case, cancer probably saved her life.

It was in her bones, and she needed chemotherapy right away, but the hospital was more than 30 miles away. She had met a husband and wife at karaoke one night months before, and friends told them about her situation—and within two days they invited her to stay in their three-room apartment near the hospital. Out of the blue, Arna had discovered a new family.

That's where she was when word of her situation reached the ear of a nonprofit group of volunteers who took on projects for elderly people in need. Jim Willard, the head of the group, scoped out the trailer to see if it could be repaired, but determined that it was far beyond help. So he started looking for an alternative and, against all odds, found one. His group had raised almost $20,000 and they used most of it to purchase a used trailer—with a working stove and refrigerator—for Arna. Then, when eighty volunteers from six local churches converged on the place, they build a ramp to accommodate Arna's growing disability, a front porch so she could enjoy her surroundings, and a rock garden. When she saw the place, she cried—and when she opened the cupboards and found them full of food, she sobbed with thankfulness.

She had a home now. The roof didn't drip water on her head, the smell of mold didn't hang in the air and the trailer had central heat to keep the chill out of her aching bones. Now all she needed, she said with a wink, was to bring some of the cats with her to keep her company. Then her family would be complete.

> Homelessness is an international problem. Poor countries and countries that have endured years of war have particularly high numbers of homeless families.

Find Out More
BOOKS

Cassidy, Jane. *Street Life: Young Women Write About Being Homeless*. London: The Women's Press, 2001.

Connolly, Deborah R. *Homeless Mothers: Face to Face with Women and Poverty*. Minneapolis: University of Minnesota Press, 2002.

Farrar-Ejemai, Brenda. *The Family in the Car: A Revelation*. Morgan Hill, Calif.: Bookstand Publishing, 2008.

Gerdes, Louise I. *The Homeless (Opposing Viewpoints)*. Chicago: Greenhaven Press, 2007.

Hubbard, Jim. *Lives Turned Upside Down: Homeless Children in Their Own Words and Photographs*. New York: Aladdin, 2007.

Kaye, Cathryn Berger. *A Kids' Guide to Hunger and Homelessness: How to Take Action!* Minneapolis: Free Spirit Publishing, 2007.

Kozol, Jonathan. *Rachel and Her Children: Homeless Families in America*. New York: Three Rivers Press, 2006.

Nunez, Ralph daCosta. *Beyond the Shelter Wall: Homeless Families Speak Out*. New York: White Tiger Press, 2004.

Nunez, Ralph daCosta. *Moving Up, Moving Out: Families Beyond Shelters*. New York: White Tiger Press, 2006.

Shankar, Lara. *Midway Station: Real-Life Stories of Homeless Children*. New York: Penguin Books, 2006.

Stronge, James H and Evelyn Reed-Victor, eds. *Educating Homeless Students: Promising Practices.* Larchmont, N.Y.: Eye on Education, 2000.

ON THE INTERNET

Habitat for Humanity International
www.habitat.org

The Homeless Families Foundation
www.homelessfamiliesfoundation.org

Homes for the Homeless
www.homesforthehomeless.com

National Alliance to End Homelessness
www.endhomelessness.org

National Center on Family Homelessness
www.familyhomelessness.org

National Coalition for the Homeless
www.nationalhomeless.org

Bibliography

Annual Homeless Assessment Report to Congress. Washington, D.C.: U.S. Department of Housing and Urban Development, Office of Community Planning and Development, 2007. Available at www.huduser.org/Publications/pdf/ahar.pdf.

Bassuk, E. L. "The Characteristics and Needs of Sheltered Homeless and Low-Income Housed Mothers." *Journal of the American Medical Association*, 276(8): 640-646, 1996.

Buckner, J. "Exposure to Violence and Low-Income Children's Mental Health." *American Journal of Orthopsychiatry*, 74(4): 413-423, 2004.

Burt, M. et al. *Homelessness: Programs and the People They Serve*. Washington, D.C.: The Urban Institute, 1999. Available at www.urbaninstitute.org.

Cauthen, N. *When Work Doesn't Pay: What Every Policymaker Should Know*. National Center for Children in Poverty, 2006. Available at www.nccp.org/publications/pub_666.html.

Culhane, J.F. "Prevalence of Child Welfare Services Involvement Among Homeless and Low-Income Mothers: A Five Year Birth Cohort Study." *Journal of Sociology and Social Welfare*, 30(3), 2003.

Grant, R. "The Health of Homeless Children Revisited." *Advances in Pediatrics*, 54(173-187), 2007.

Grant, R. "Asthma Among Homeless Children in New York City: An Update." *American Journal of Public Health*, 97(3): 448-450, 2007.

Joint Center for Housing Studies of Harvard University. *The State of the Nation's Housing*, 2007. Available at ww.jchs.harvard.edu/publications/markets/son2007/son2007_bw.pdf.

Kids Count, Annie E. Casey Foundation. Available at www.kidscount.org/datacenter/profile_results.jsp?d=1&r=1.

Li, H. *The Changing Demographics of Low-Income Families and Their Children* (Living At the Edge Research Brief #2). New York: National Center for Children in Poverty, 2003. Available at www.nccp.org/publications/pdf/text_529.pdf.

National Child Traumatic Stress Network. *Facts on Trauma and Homeless Children*. 2005. Available at www.nctsnet.org/nctsn_assets/pdfs/promising_practices/Facts_on_Trauma_and_Homeless_Children.pdf.

National Low-Income Housing Coalition. *Out of Reach 2008*. Available at www.nlihc.org.

Office of Elementary and Secondary Education. *Report to the President and Congress on the Implementation of the Education for Homeless Children and Youth Program Under the McKinney-Vento Homeless Assistance Ac*t. Washington, D.C.: U.S. Department of Education, 2006. Available at www.ed.gov.

Schwarz, K.B. "High Prevalence of Overweight and Obesity in Homeless Baltimore Children and Their Caregivers: A Pilot Study." *Clinical Nutrition and Obesity*, 9(1): 48, 2007.

U. S. Conference of Mayors. *Hunger and Homelessness Survey*. 2006. Available at www.usmayors.org.

Waldron, T. *Working Hard, Falling Short: America's Working Families and the Pursuit of Economic Security.* Annie E. Casey Foundation, 2004. Available at http://www.aecf.org/upload/publicationfiles/working%20hard.pdf.

Weinreb, L. "A Comparison of the Health and Mental Health Status of Homeless Mothers in Worcester, Mass: 1993 and 2003." *American Journal of Public Health*, 96(8): 1444-1448, 2006.

Index

About the Author and the Consultant

AUTHOR

Julianna Fields is the pseudonym of a Gannett human interest columnist whose byline has also appeared in *Writer's Digest*, *American History*, *American Woodworker* and hundreds of other publications, as well as educational workbooks and a guidebook about Steamtown, a National Park Service site in Scranton, Pennsylvania. She's also a writing coach and editor.

CONSULTANT

Gallup has studied human nature and behavior for more than seventy years. Gallup's reputation for delivering relevant, timely, and visionary research on what people around the world think and feel is the cornerstone of the organization. Gallup employs many of the world's leading scientists in management, economics, psychology, and sociology, and its consultants assist leaders in identifying and monitoring behavioral economic indicators worldwide. Gallup consultants help organizations boost organic growth by increasing customer engagement and maximizing employee productivity through measurement tools, coursework, and strategic advisory services. Gallup's 2,000 professionals deliver services at client organizations, through the Web, at Gallup University's campuses, and in forty offices around the world.